Say The Silence

SAY THE SILENCE

© 1997 by Doreen Gandy Wiley

Published by Celilo Publications

3021 S.W. Florida Street, Portland, Oregon 97219-1834

(Available for $10.95)

FIRST EDITION

LIBRARY OF CONGRESS Catalogue Card Number: 96-092831

ISBN: 0-9614529-1-9

Cover photo of Mori Point, Pacifica, California by Doreen Gandy Wiley.

Back cover photo of the author by Donna Chainas.

Design and production by LRF Designs.

Other books by Doreen Gandy Wiley

Poetry:

Sing the Day (1972)
Miracle Publications, LaGrande, Oregon (o.p.)

Poems for Twelve Moods (1979) Dragon's Teeth Press,
Georgetown, California

A New Leafing, A Journey from Grief (1985)
Celilo Publications, Portland, Oregon

Fiction:

Fires of Survival (1995)
Strawberry Hill Press, Portland, Oregon

Say The Silence

It flows
though I cannot see it,
like your voice
singing the silence
in the channels of my mind.

Poems by
Doreen Gandy Wiley

For Beth,
This book comes to you
as a gift from your Mom.
We both wish you a
very special, happy
birthday!
Doreen Gandy Wiley
October 25, 1999

Celilo Publications
3021 S.W Florida Street
Portland, Oregon 97219-1834

Acknowledgments

Grateful acknowledgment is made to the following publications where the poems listed below first appeared. Thanks are due the editors for permission to reprint:

A New Leafing, A Journey From Grief, Celilo Publications: *Recipe from an Oyster*; The Archer: *Seventh Birthday, Sonnet for Mark, You Cannot Grow a Garden in the Shade, Methuselah's Refrain, Two in One, Respite on the Rogue, Tell it on the Water, River Dream, Columbia Ice Fields, Ethel by the Pond, Spring Brew, Sea Music*; Assemblage, Oregon State Poetry Association Collection: *A Branch to Brace a Fishing Pole*; At The Bell's Quick Sound–A Tribute to Sr. Helena Brand,(1915-1995)©1997: *A Walk Along the Puget Sound;* Encore Magazine: *St. Francis of the Sea*; Hibiscus Magazine: *Collision Course, While Scaling the Salmon—Mozart's Concerto in C for Oboe*; Green's Magazine (Canada): *Bass Player, Ephedra, Old Buffalo at Yellowstone, On the Road to Ramsey Canyon, Brahms for Breakfast, John Steinbeck's Salinas Valley, Open Window in Bear Country, The Old Coin Collector, Beyond the Desert's Eye, Haiku, Secrets of the Chiracahuas, Takeover*; In Our Own Voices, Vol. 4– Oregon Writers' Colony: *Not Before Its Time*; In Our Own Voices, Vol. 5– *Ice Tree*; The Lyric: *Twice-Brewed Tea*; Moose, a Magazine of Portland: *Impressions on Utamaro's Woodblock 'Okita Carrying a Teacup', Bird Refuge at Arch Cape*; Poet Trails: *The Observer*; Shorelines, The Newsguard: *The Worry Bird, Half a Prize*; The Portland Pen, National League of American Pen Women: *All Day Has Felt Like Sunday, Unspoken Minds, Shenandoah*; The Willamette Writer: *Cactus Salute*.

The following poems have won contest awards: The Archer Poetry Contest: *You Cannot Grow a Garden in the Shade*, Third Place, 1993; National Federation of State Poetry Societies, California Award: *Canyon Raid*, First Place, 1982; Oregon Association of American Mothers Poetry Contest: *The Mannequin*, Second Place, 1989; *Empty House*, Second Place, 1987; The Portland Pen, National League of American Pen Women Contest: *Eye of the Diamond*, First Place, 1987; *Shared Intimacy*, Second Place, 1987; *Unspoken Minds*, Second Place, 1986; Writer's Digest Poetry Contest: *A Threatened Species*, Finalist, 1991.

The following poem was presented at a reading in The Governor's Ceremonial Office: Northwest Poetry and Prose—In Thanksgiving, November 9, 1988: *Respite on the Rogue*.

With pleasure and gratitude, I thank Marlene Howard and Barbara Drake for their generous written comments. Jean-Louis Brindamour for his support and guidance; my daughter, Gigi Wood, for reviewing the manuscript; my husband, Joe, for his love and support; and Loretta Ruth Fisher for design and production.

This book is dedicated to my grandchildren:
Ryan, Nolan, Mark, Rachel, Emily, Justin and Austin
in the hope that these poems
will have meaning for them.

Contents

I. *A Garden of Faces*

The world is so empty if one thinks
only of mountains, rivers and cities;
but to know someone who thinks and
feels with us, and who, though distant,
is close to us in spirit, this makes
the earth for us an inhabited garden.

Goethe
1749-1832

1. *Life Line*

Traveling in the company
of those we love is home
in motion.

Leigh Hunt
1784-1859

Life Line

When my mother's arms became too full to hold me,
I hung onto the hem of her skirt and followed
like a loose rudder. In her wake,
I learned to survive ambivalent tides,
ride on runaway currents.
Held too tightly in my mother's arms, two younger brothers,
mouths open into a stinging spray, screamed,
while she fought for balance on a tipsy ship—land, home
snatched away—made exile by the man she married.

Her journey became mine: My choice, to hold onto
the hard edge of her skirt, an umbilicus from which
cut-off meant destruction.
Leaning from the deck's cold rail, she longed for
the drowning reach of the waves, but tugs and pulls
against her body, hard as those of the unborn,
anchored her to the deck of the proven steamer, as
on a gigantic shark's fin, she rode the peaks of the stormy
Atlantic to the sun-split shores of the Mediterranean.
A narcotic calm harbored us in. I let go, to link with
tanned arthritic hands and soft broad breasts.
My brothers stopped screaming.

It was mother who rode a five-year tide
before she could release that Neptune face she loved
to the amorphous deep. Even then, she followed it,
a Nereid in an underwater dream that pulled her into
black hole caverns of an ocean galaxy for long
clandestine moments in a watery tomb. Until one summer day
when orange blossoms colored the air with scent, she
surfaced—limp, indifferent, never ready; but staring
at a swarthy sun. And I, consoled by the sweet babble
of elders, stood by, hands loose at my sides,
aware of the hard little hem of her skirt
as it hit her calves when she walked.

Sun At My Back

Grandmother Teresa smiled at me,

arranged the sun at my back,

gifted me a confidence I pocketed for life.

She sat me beside her on a stool,

placed two whittled lollipop sticks in my hands

and showed me how to knit   purl one   knit one…

I felt her heartbeat drumming in my hands.

Seventh Birthday—1934
for Bert

In Rudy Valle's songs

I heard your classy voice,

saw your wavy hair, arched nose.

I jigged

to notes so debonaire,

until the needle THUNKED

on the 78-record.

Ride The Running Board
for Uncle Ovidio

Was it a '34 Nash or a '33 Packard?
I can't remember.
All I recall of Uncle Ovidio's black sedan
was its looming shine, white-walled tires
that spun so fast they waxed smooth;
and the winged creature with silver breasts, who rode
the hood like the guardian lady on a galleon's prow.
He polished her tenderly with a soft flannel cloth.
"No touch!" he'd warn in marginal English.
Uncle was from sheepherder country in the Basque mountains.
We suspected he'd never had much schooling,
but when he polished that fine sedan, he'd tune
the shortwave to the New York Yankees
and never miss a play they made.

His brow, smooth as paper, he communicated through
scrutiny of muted hazel eyes, the Havana cigar
he puffed blowing the most perfect smoke rings.
When he called "Ride!" we'd jump around the car
as he signalled where we were to sit—often
five or six of us—brothers, sisters, cousins—until
we packed in, all elbows and knees.
Those left got to ride the running board.
"Jus' to the corner," he'd wave, and we would move
at ten miles an hour to the yellow ice cream cart
that belled its presence twice a day.

I never understood why he let us eat the cones
and ice cream pies, a deadly threat
to the grey velvet upholstery, and the tasseled curtains,
which I loved to flick.
"No touch!" he'd bark, though we could hear
a buried chuckle in his staunch command.
Hands in the air, we would pile in—chocolate moustaches,
strawberry fingers and vanilla mouths—then sit
in silence, hands folded.

When I lagged behind and got to ride the running board,
I felt the breeze lift my hair, and my heart pound
above the rumble of the motor. Too soon, Uncle would stop,
get out—the others waiting in the car—come over
and give me a hug as he lifted me down.
He never wiped my sticky kisses from his cheek.

A Favorite Aunt

a year after her death in the Philippines

Being with Auntie Teresita felt like being home—
special, as the children she never had,
because "the world was too cruel a place."
There was something of that loss in her touch,
like feathers brushing your chin,
or a pat so light on your shoulder
you sensed she felt you might disappear.

It was her eyes that verified your place.
Held in her dark gaze, you knew you were as unique
as she said you were. (A shock to learn later
that all your cousins felt that way.)

If by accident you marred her teakwood table,
or spilled Ceylon tea on a prized China rug,
she'd scold like a mother crane, straining
a slender neck so her chignon trembled, and her
Spanish nose probed straight into your sin.
Just when your heart leaped in remorse, flecks
fired in her eyes, relieving you of major crime.
Minutes later, your sandaled feet dangled
from her best mahogany chair.

She'd lift a bowl of fruit, throwing reflected rings
on an immense brass coffee table—mango yellow,
tangerine, grape green, lanzone gold.
She feasted on the ritual: Her laugh vibrated
under the silk yolk of a favorite lavender blouse.
You couldn't stop the giggle that raced up from
your toes as you reached for the tender treat she held.
The fruit was always runny/sweet, and Auntie Teresita
watched you try to slurp the juice before it dribbled
downward, laughter shining in her eyes.

For El Capitán

The father's ashes are scattered wide
over this Eden of rock.
I discern his face in the granite monarch, El Capitán;
listen to the music of the Merced River
      sing out his name.
He is one with the imponderable peace of the water;
from glacial sands, flinting with mica, he spirals
      with the brawny red-barked pine.
I hear him in the one-note song
      of a hidden bird, and in
      the regal swish of a gray squirrel's tail.

He sleeps on a bed of pine needles
scattered over this forest floor; he hears
the dry rain of needles falling forever
      on his sleep.

Sleep, El Capitán,
dream your deepest dream.

Disclosure In Late Afternoon

I look into the mirror and see my aunt's smile.
Because she was said to be the prettiest
of the five sisters, it pleases me.
But I remember Maria, who nurtured bounties
of multi-flora roses, dahlias big as dinner plates,
cloying honeysuckle, and iris with lavender petals
and sunfilled cups.

What of her touch at sickbeds, with night
her only companion, when polio was a threat
in every ache and fever.

Late this afternoon I found her rust-eaten trowel,
held its paint-stripped handle. Rescued
her China hat, sun-baked, its black ties raveling.
They hid there, under the sag of shelves
in the greenhouse, untouched except for
a drape of dusty cobwebs.

I contemplate a blue jay scattering beechnuts,
and watch the wind tell a canopy of leaves
above me how to sway. A gust brings
the honest aroma of newly turned compost,
dried grasses, myriad scents from her garden.
I recognize, as hers, the hand I raise to shield
my eyes from the split light of a declining sun.

Dream At The Edge Of Sunrise

"Row, row, row your boat..."

They come into the dreaming night
with muddy boots, soldiers from battle.
One I recognize. He has been dead for years.
In a letter he once signed himself, "Eternally yours."
I am dreaming him alive.

Images of deer, transparent as glass, appear
in the clouds. There are no deer here, nor
in the sleeping woods. They are dreaming themselves.

Snakes, wrapped like boas around the legs,
were left in the walk from the field.
They escaped mines buried in new grass.

The soldiers abandon their guns,
manage the river without oars. He is one of them.
Light seeps under a horizon of darkness.
It is but day intruding upon a dream.
I lift away from a night that has invented itself
and enter a dreaming day.

Gatita

1978-1992

Gatita would come when I felt most alone, to fill
those moments when out of the corner of my eye, I
kept her presence visible—a twitch of an attentive ear,
an opening of moon-green eye, a purr from across
her fur-warmed orange chair. She was there.

Now the memory of her haunts a tail glint
I still see and brush of calico I still feel.
She has become a mutable shadow that cannot
warm the corner that was solely hers.

J A Z Z

Your name was meant for you.
There was certain music in your run,
      ears flapping in an ambient autumn wind,
      raindrops glistening on mahogany-brown coat,
      your nose wet with elation,
      saucy chocolate eyes roaming everywhere. . .

You lived your life like a pup, Jazz,
lured by hidden backwood paths, ever
on the edge of some discovery,
disobeying fences, stern commands—
you had your day!

Tender friend, your deep forgiving heart
was loyal to the bone, ferocious to any stranger's step.
You were a bedtime nuzzler to the two who loved you most,
cradlewatcher to the tiniest bundles, first Mark—
then Rachel—vigilant, while the household
softly snored the hours till dawn.

How could you be released from life without
stirring abject grief in those of us you loved
without restraint?
      We hear your lively music in rhythms we won't give up,
      consoled by memory echoes that bring you back,
reminding us your pilgrim heart has found
its final solace and its peace.

Empty House

My house is empty now; I must move on.
Family portraits from these walls are gone,
leave squares imprinted in a timeless dye.

The cry that's pitched so thinly is my cry,
a plea for words and deeds not done,
for actions failed and candid hearts foregone.

Each square still holds a face I call upon
to share a past that claims us, everyone,
and thereby let old devils finally die!

It's time to harvest fruit, fine wheat and rye,
and when we're through, be like the geese and fly
to new directions in a changing sky.

2. *I Know Your Face*

A portrait clear as
diamond rain caught in
a waterfall of leaves.

I Know Her Face
for Rachel

I know the secret of her face,
this child, in birth just once removed;
first sculpted from the thighs of two
stone lovers joined in a Rodin pose.

The face of Rachel
born through me once before,
now of my daughter's being—waters
from a trident headspring
resonating life.

I know this babe,
skin soft as dandelion's breath,
eyes caught in a perpetual smile,
nose nuzzled as a lamb's,
upturned in promise dignified,
as is her pointed chin.

Her heartbeat fast against my breast,
her sighs return the years
from dimly focused past: a portrait
clear as diamond rain caught
in a waterfall of leaves.

Her father strums strong rhythms,
brightening his young son's face, caressing
my daughter's pensive eyes,
each note a song in Rachel's heart.

Daughter Of The Autumn Light
  for Gigi

Caught in camera lens
      vine maple fire behind
      the toasted softness of your hair,
      burnish ivory satin in your cheeks,
      torch reflections into depth of sage green eyes.
      (Not in the picture, the old pumpkin,
      dethroned on compost pile, its
      halloween face, a sagging orange mask.)

Daughter of the autumn light,
      girl-sky no longer blue, purified
      by changing winds, obscured by raging clouds,
      still gently rooted.

Woman now,
      hands textured as these leaves,
      gristle-veined by birth and slow dying—your
      hands lifting infants from their cribs,
      lighting candles to their darkened cries,
      turning the soil of many gardens, from which
      you have returned—seeded, lost and reborn.

Woman now,
      the girl who scattered dew into my mornings—gone,
      her laughter echoing pain,
      her forehead furrowed by a plowline wrested
      from the earth.

Now woman in the autumn light,
      you touch the winter in my heart.

Relevancy

Glued impossibly to a crumbling sheet
in a family album, a black and white print
of father, daughter and dog, sitting
on a bank above a field of horses. A question rides
on the daughter's nose, though her eyes stay fixed
on the vision below—the waving manes, the dancing
hooves on a lace of shadows and daisies.
Fenced in, she sees the horses free and yearns to ride.
Not yet, says the incline of his head, though
his eyes protect the dream. He leans toward her,
just enough to reveal the comfortable drape
of a checkered cotton shirt he wears on weekends.
She knows to trust his word. It was the same
with the shaggy Shetlands before she rode them all,
in a long procession of seasons.

The snapshot has been lost in the album for years.
Rediscovered, she wants it now, enlarged and framed,
so she can see more clearly—the daisies forever
ticking across the grass, embroidering the horses' hooves,
riding across the golden paws of the spaniel sitting
beside them, tongue perpetually panting; and they,
unfettered in a field returned—her father and herself.

From Lights Within

Trailing clouds of glory do we come from God who is our home.

William Wordsworth

Declaring their perfume without restraint,
a garden of bosomy roses
like a group of attentive midwives, while
red-feathered sumacs burn
           under the worried O
           of a late September moon.

At daybreak
those high-rollers, the poplars,
           leaves clinking like coins,
           bet on a boy!

In the birthing room
Mozart's horn concerto swells its prayer,
surging its vibratos through wide windows
to the brassy cymbals of the sulphur yellow poplars.

Crescendoing
riptides within   she bears down
                           without a cry,
                           her heart beating
                           like a star.

      Breaking loose
      through his mother's thighs
      down the channel
      he comes,
          a little salmon
          tight
    on a silver
              c
              o
              r
              d

Sonnet For Mark

When I enter the room to be with Mark,
I meet his welcome eyes, unswerving blue,
that follow every move I make, and spark
to every word I say (all other sounds eschew).
A captivating smile says, "Here, come here!"
Because I relish rapturous display,
I signal him to "wait a minute, dear."
It's so delicious to prolong, delay
anticipation so complete, so pure.
When finally I reach his waiting arms,
he pats my hand and offers swift allure.
With wreathing smiles my very heart disarms.
Enslaved to this sweet seal who drums the floor—
my grandson, Mark! I could not ask for more.

The Mannequin

For him the mannequin has power.

Her hand extended, she looms

five feet above him, all curls

and feverish eyes, and nose

as sharp as glass.

He gazes up at beads

that form a clinking lei

around her pallid neck,

reflecting glints of red

into his wide-eyed awe,

his own curls soft around

his oval face.

He waits ten seconds,

then taking her hard fingers

into his, shoots

a purposed voice up

to her crimson smile:

Please move!" he says,

and stands and waits

for a glittered eye to blink.

Song Of Evening
for Maggie

Enclosed inside, the shell has light.

It moves like the wind over sand

lifting specks of fine gold dust.

Far in the darkness, a line of blue

marks the water.

It flows

though I cannot see it,

like your voice

singing the silence

in the channels of my mind.

A Separate Beat

The brothers are towheads,

    both tall, lean, blue-eyed.

The elder describes an incident:

    "It happened in a second."

The younger scratches his head:

    "Was it a short second or a long second?"

The elder frowns:

    "A second is a second!"

The younger cocks his head and presses his fist to his chin.

Portrait Of An Old Apple

I never thought I looked that old.
My eyes, Nolan, so sunken in your sketch,
my lips in a dream smile, barely saving me
from looking like E.T.'s grandmother!
Yet, I am astounded by your rendering of wrinkles,
tender touches worked by magic eye. You,
a mere nine years.

You capture once smooth skin branded by
summer laughter, winter loss,
that wind-whipped hair, and, ah, the trace
of royalty in Mediterranean cheekbones,
stony Scottish chin—all there.

You return me to the cave, Nolan,
create me, a watchful crone, flashing
survival in eyes as deep as caverns,
leading to tribal birth chambers,
from where your own wail once began.

Are you my torchbearer then,
daring the grist mill of generations
through mysterious insights, truths
I hardly know about myself?

Will this gift with which you weigh me
be returned, when future grandchild sees
beyond your eyes to render your old apple face
and blatantly reveal that you are edging seventy?

Crest Like Eagles

Surprise Dinner

We climb to the horseshoe overlook at Cathedral Point.
Circled by glacial fingerwork at 8000 feet,
we are led up a spare path, flanked by marbled
rock—icy white, pink, fiery rust—to a peak
in a rimless sky, a point singular, yet abstract.

They have prepared a table for us:
Chicken, rice, wine, and roses on a pink cloth.
But the gifts they serve consist of a feeling
in his eyes, a caress in her voice.

Our mountain minstrel sings of love,
sends us tapering to where wind
is kin to God and breathing clouds.

Rainbows For Lisa

A gray day, misted
as seagull's flight through ocean fog;
an hour for mourning
brought on by rain's sharp sting
that cannot be erased by thoughts
of brighter days, when sunlight
flooded your life with laughter,
in lakeside water play, on hikes
up western canyons, and, later, in
fireside pleasures after rich gatherings
with those who loved you for what you were—
a Peter Pan, a maverick heart whose
unique energy pulled beyond the depth
of haunting hazel eyes: Your beauty, Lisa, equal
to a fawn's soft grace by silent forest pools.

You saved scores of injured pups and kittens,
but could not save yourself, except
by exiting the mortal pain.
You had to go, it was your choice;
but, oh, the fires of love you left still burning...

Our only touchstone now
is in a rainbow's bridge: We force ourselves
to recognize the storm has passed for you.
For us, so difficult to face that small bright jewel
that remains your essence,
headed away to rainbows still invisible,
as is your touch in arcs of rising color.

The Wooden Shell

for my son on his thirtieth birthday

The beauty of the handcarved wooden shell
is synthesis of forests and of seas,
of blended elements that clearly tell
the birth of oceans carved from roughhewn trees:
Like the evolvement of your tender life
at once so full of innocence and care,
then chiseled out by pain and cutting strife,
repeated misdirection and despair.

Today, a whole and balanced form appears,
carved from your heart and rendered by your hands,
through a belief in self, a faith that clears
the terror that once held in iron bands.

Thirty rings now shine in your tall tree,
a climbing spire by gusty oceans—free!

Carvings On The Heart
for Rich

Years fall—caesuras caught in canyon walls
slabbed like dominoes around Lake Billy Chinook.

Shimmers of memory ride stars through juniper.
The scene is sweet as lavender purpling dusky air,
fair as wheat waving from fields beyond the stony rim:

>   *Through shadows forged by campfire,*
>   *I see you, a flush-cheeked boy,*
>   *intent on roasting perfect marshmallows.*
>   *We followed deer and raccoon tracks*
>   *around an open grate. Your laughter rang*
>   *high over stubble sage, lifted over*
>   *slapping waters of the lake.*

Tomorrow, you will fold the faded tent, match
each crease into long lines of wear, haul
the chipped red lantern down, lift it
by the chain your father linked.
You will roll the tent into his tough old Navy bag;
the chain, you'll lay in his dented gear box
by an assembly of tools, gritty from a quarter
century of use.

An owl echoes over crickets' croon.
Starlight softens the canyon's hard fall. Over
a circle of voices, the campfire snaps, billows
its heat on our bare shins, makes our eyes burn.

I gaze at your man's face—molded cheekbones, fine nose,
thoughtful eyes, and I feel the chronic ache ease:
This is your time. Mine, memory's sacred writ.

Apologia To Army Hill

Mother sat by the upstairs window
under a curl of woodsmoke. She leaned
into her easel and brushed swirls of leaves
onto the slopes of Army Hill, where
we played war on the banks of cottonwoods
and fir spires, so tall they punctured clouds.

She mixed fast-drying paints—dabs of Naples yellow
for turning leaves, burnt umber for bark
of the occasional oak, vermillion red for vine maples,
and veridian green for the banks, lots of veridian green.

She was deaf to the clangor of our makeshift weapons
as we charged up and down the hill. Her eyes
caressed the canvas. She stroked each leaf, trunk,
and twig with an anxious brush.

She left us out—our heated faces, our lips purple as
rigor mortis from the comsumption of too many blackberries.
Our hair parted by wind, we played into the long-fingered
afternoon, while she dab-dabbled at her scene.

For supper we had thrice-left-over-stew.

She propped the canvas on the kitchen counter when she
finished it, up high, where it stared hard at us for
a solid week. Never saw it again until yesterday.
She surprised me for my thirtieth. There it was—
the tawny scene—framed in varnished oak under lack-lustre glass.

"It will look fine above your couch," she said, meaning
the new couch, mostly flowered blue (very little tawny
and no veridian).

"It's Army Hill," I said, fingering the cool glass.
Mother nodded and said nothing more, but as she held
my gaze, I saw my image, painted clearly in her eyes.

She'll Sing You Songs Without Reserve
for Emily

She is a Mary Cassatt child,
> with Renoir curls that frame
> her cherub cheeks, heighten her
> eyes, blue as summer sapphires.

The petaled face of this small explorer
> is enhanced by an inner bounce that
> emanates from a driving curiosity.

She'll announce all she knows, then
> sing you songs without reserve,
> tunes you once knew well, but now
> wish you could preserve just as
> as she sings them, each note
> remembered in the heart.

A Dance For Emily

The last to leave the party, they
lingered in the kitchen, picking
at the chips and carrots. Emily
came in with a white plastic bow
from a package, asked me to put it
in her hair, then ran to show
her mother. A half minute later,
she bounced into a conversation
I was having with her father.
"Dance with me, Daddy," she tugged
at his hand, her head at his thigh.
"Later, Emmy," he told her, unaware
of the plea in her eyes.

She made two wide turns around the table,
then sidled up again. Her head
to one side, eyes raised once more,
"I have a pretty bow in my hair, Daddy.
Please dance with me now."

Her voice stopped him this time.
In one enchanted sweep, he caught her up
and held her in his arms.
They danced slowly to a phantom waltz.
I could only see her eyes, reflecting
the grin she buried in his shoulder,
as they swept past, slightly blurred,
on the mahogany mirror of the table,
the white bow triumphant in her hair.

Winner
  cinquain for Justin

You fly,
a meteor
down the sun-washed mountain,
charge ahead of all the others—
trophy!

Meandering Road

Going on April and the redwinged blackbird
swoons over fields of wild mustard,
throws his shifty shadow over yellow reflections
brimming in the swampy estuary.

Clouds sing above us as we travel home.
Birthday children await, their arms open,
their eager fingers reach to intertwine
with ours, their voices lilt in the rush
of tight embraces and gummy kisses
of the very young.

How long away we've traveled:
      Old rivers meander,
      the Rio Grande, the Sacramento . . .

Desert miles left behind, we have traded
dry winds and yucca for fir-rich mountains
and misty rain: the Northwest slows our minds,
races the beat of our hearts to join with
children's voices, burbling freshets,
proclaiming we never really left.

Last Of The Neighborhood Kids

Beth got married today. She did it
with a flourish of shocking pink, white
satin and lace, an eye-level cake,
and music that sweetened our ears.

Through the candle light
that angelized her face, I saw the kid
who played street ball with a riotous bunch
that drifted aside like autumn leaves
to let impatient cars go past.

She stormed off sometimes, little sister,
sun-burnished hair flying and prideful nose
in the air. Beth was tough. On Halloween,
she joined the best of them, draping
toilet paper around the thin-barked birch,
which still bears surgery of initials carved,
and hearts outlined in blackened sap.

Bandaids on scabby knees, hanging by magic,
she shinnied up the copper beech to reign
over a swirl of falling leaves that still mirror
dozens of bright faces—braids, crewcuts,
banded teeth, frosty noses. . .

Leaves lift in the wind, carry their voices—those
who left, grew up, moved away or died.

A rain of years falls on a neighborhood
anesthetized mostly by grandparent types
and a few younger ones. You could say
Beth was the last of the baby boomers.
She's everybody's kid. Married today,
but she'll be back like the red-gold squirrel
who shows up every fall in search of harvest
in the trees.

We'll hear his chitter among the leafy faces
of children gone, blending with their voices
in whispers of wind.

3. *You Cannot Grow A Garden*
   In The Shade

   Fail to nourish and surely you'll degrade
the chemistry of life, and nothing gain,
no matter how you shovel or you spade.

You Cannot Grow A Garden In The Shade
villanelle

No matter how you shovel or you spade
without the sun your work will be in vain;
you cannot grow a garden in the shade.

Neither can the flowers you plant be made
to reach maturity in poor terrain,
no matter how you shovel or you spade.

Likewise, if friends for flowers we were to trade,
and sunlight's sustenance for love's pure strain,
we could not grow a garden in the shade.

Fail to nourish and surely you'll degrade
the chemistry of life, and nothing gain,
no matter how you shovel or you spade.

Cease to cultivate and watch health fade,
replacing nourishment with abject pain;
you cannot grow a garden in the shade.

So if you want your plantings green as jade,
and friendships flourishing as new sprung grain,
no matter how you shovel or you spade,
you must not grow a garden in the shade.

The Visit

Her gray-green eyes
reflect a muted twilight best;
tell you to come just so close,
offer aloof invitation
to contemplate
the minutes before dark
when sunset leaves
its subtle purple streaks,
and the world lowers
to meet her quiet voice.

She pulls you in softly
with agile fingers
eager for your thoughts.
Catlike, she plays with your words,
turning them over and over
until they are quite dead.

When you leave
                  your footsteps
                       remain luminous
                            on her white rug.

Eye Of A Diamond

With you I entered the eye of a diamond,
fancying my worth in multiple reflections.
Refulgent as cathedral glass,
I shimmered every time you passed.
As you enlarged the magnitude of light,
I followed with a spectrummed night,
sure there was no end to prisms.

The eye of the diamond is a prison.
Now in morning plainness,
gone is diamond brightness.
Closed the eye! You take your dazzling
elsewhere, leaving me as unreflective
as the air.

Still I marvel at your capture
of transparencies, knowing
the carat always remains yours.

Collision Course

He
is an open triangle.
She,
a speeding parallelogram—
the space between them
nullified.

Even when
she tunnels through him,
she never touches.

Impressions On Utamaro's Woodblock
Okita Carrying a Teacup

Under black pagoda of hair
your face, a blanched almond;
in boneless fingers you carry a teacup
      light as a thimble
to that part of the picture
we do not see: the edge of your
silk-flowered kimono
blunted by square fingers.
Words lift with aroma of tea
      are nimbly turned into pearls.
In a low bend, you pour the tea.
Through a wall of paper
      scissors of rain
      in curled petals
of lavender chrysanthemums.

The Observer
cinquain

Old gate

forgotten, hides

in green entanglement

and watches through a wooden eye—

the world.

A Walk Along The Puget Sound
Centrum Conference—1977

Through a frame in memory,
you and I walk along the Sound.
I lengthen my steps to keep up
with your sensible strides,
purposeful as your mind, your
eyes never missing peripheral view
of birds' flight over darkening waters
to Whidbey's quiet shore, a short channel
away from your Seattle birthplace.

A round of memories surfaces—of father,
mother, sister, brothers. The eldest,
you set out in quest of excellence,
"Aimed for the stars," and, yes, attained
the largest measure of your goals.

Certain people, you acknowledged, found
your ardor unforgiving. (You recognized
that mantle about you, which distanced
some as if they had encountered armor, while
others found you inspirational as the stars
for which you reached.)

I, on the other hand, relive that walk
along the Sound, strain to hear your words,
which come like shadow's song, soft as down
from a gull's wing, swooping to the water
before the overtaking night: "Please stay awhile
and walk with me."

Bass Player

His consolation
is the bass he plays
for the banjo band.
Memories of her
thump from the belly
of his instrument.

>   A deep ache
>   pulses
>   from its hollow shell.

He hates it
when the music stops.

Weathervane
cinquain

Clear days

are beckoning,

gleam like polished brass;

but it takes clouds to make a good

sunset.

The Worry Bird

When you worry
be like a bird on a nest,
feathers spread over warm
sweet smell of grasses woven
around and under,
drowsy as you listen to summer
birdsong filtering through
blossoms of an old apple tree.
Sitting on your worries—those
personally cultivated eggs—
safe under your warmth,
nurture those fears,
anxieties, the little terrors
that you breed.
And there, under your feathers
they will wait, until you wake—
so well cared for!

Forward Look
cinquain

You cried

a litany,

recalling all past ills.

Listen! That was then; this is now.

Forget.

Methuselah's Refrain

sonnet

It's not enough for fledgling hearts to know
that ultimately everything must fail,
eternal night will darken this whole show;
there's not a one whom time will not assail.
Not blamed for its indifference,
youth's special world does not include
the cares of age and death; and hence,
rejects the onslaught of decrepitude.

Yet from the young the gift one might expect
is love, if not the spur to empathize;
intention to relate and not reject,
eventually coming to realize
we're drumming to Methuselah's refrain,
for who will ever pass sixteen again?

II *Probing the Heart*

There is no companion but love
no starting, no finishing, yet a
road.

Rumi
Persian Poet
1207-1273

Twice-brewed Tea

We have found
the second go-around
is like twice-brewed tea:
initially shared, it's easy to see
after being served once more,
what remains is honest flavor—
the bite, the flare—
which selectively aware,
distinctive tongues can savor.

Not Before Its Time

Falling in love was a rush over a waterfall,
a kite over treetops, a celestial high.
Mellow after eight years, I drift
on my own thoughts, sit as if you were not here,
spooning your cereal beside me, telling me
how you would run the government.
I watch the fog shroud the kitchen window;
talk about the weather is hot enough for me.

You say I waffle; I say that you're unswerving.
          I like to pot geraniums, water indoor violets;
          you turn compost heaps, inhale the pungent fumes,
          and breathe, "I love the smell of earth."
Am I the dreamer, then? You, feet on the ground?
          You're gentle as a fawn when the grandkids nuzzle;
          debonaire, when you make me dazzle, saying,
          "You're a number in that dress."
Some days we are as distant as Pluto is to Venus, yet
we can contemplate a sunset till the sky turns dark as lead.
And when you hold my hand before we drift to sleep,
          I can't unbend your fingers,
               or tell whose hand is whose.

Shared Intimacy

You smell like
wet chicken feathers when
you come in from fixing
the ruptured pipe.
I pull my chair next
to your rocker.
     Small drops of water shine
     on the collar of your red shirt.
     "Did you fix the leak?"
You stare ahead.
All you want is to have
me sit here,
     while
         you
    rock.

Ephedra

Boiling sulphur pool, Ephedra,
furious blue
like your eyes
when you raged at me last night
for denting the screen door
of the trailer. I should have
remembered to move the sliding plate—
that hateful metal square—and you
should have reined your anger.
      "How many times have I told you
      to slide that plate before you close
      the door; but you insist, you just insist!"
I, like Ephedra then
in this wondrous Yellowstone,
boiled over, too.
      "I am a person. That is a door!"
My indignation branded hard into your heart,
while you changed moods and played
sage advocate to sanity.
Released in soft winds of the night,
the anger passed,
and like the pool
in moments of cooling,
we sit in the sun,
feet propped on a warm rock,
drinking coffee,
shadows from sweet-smelling pines
fingering our hair.

The Old Buffalo at Yellowstone

The old buffalo at the park
reminds me of you in your rocker.
He makes a circle of security
in the soft dirt,
settling down and down
until he is quite comfortable.
Then he sits and dozes;
his breathing lifts
the hulking mountain of his coat.
His eyes lower under shaggy brows...
his thoughts are his own.
He twitches occasionally at flies
buzzing in a halo of fine dust
that settles on the hunch of his back.

Do I see his head move rhythmically
as yours does when you nod
in your rocker?

All Day It Felt Like Sunday

I wait for some unscheduled thing
        to happen, but
you away,
        I'm much too unsymmetrical
        to function well at anything...
Monotony of rain
        opens on reflections
        in a deeper eye, a recessed pain:
Fresh replay of summer—
        sun-scorch
        on juniper and pine,
light dozing off your face,
        sparks in your eyes.
In tight embrace
        our bodies stretch,
        nude in sleeping bags.
We taste salt off each other's shoulders,
        our sighs lengthen into slumber.
At our heads
        a lulling creek clocks years
over waterworn rocks.

On The Road To Ramsey Canyon

The orange we divide is moist
on our tongues. You love this desert
as if you belong here—your roughhewn
profile could be carved
in the rocks behind you,
could blend and disappear into them.
I like you in this country,
your eyes are undiluted as the Western sky,
torched by yuccas blooming white
in gardens of the sun, and honest
as horizons roamed by Cochise tribes.

Naked rocks ring an illusion of a once-real ocean,
still pulling shades of blue across believing eyes.

In Ramsey Canyon
white-tailed deer spirit through bleached sycamore...

Look at these mountains!
They have not changed in eons:
Ridged mesas balance on ledge of sky,
warriors of the great upheaval,
translators of time.

In this jarred creation,
a soft sense.

Morning Too Bright
a salute to W.H. Auden

Did I love you too much last night
      in thirst to excess?
Will midday sun that brains the hills
      melt me with mortal heat? I

leave you dozing.

A thief with an encumbering burden, I
      take jittery steps
down dawn-painted fields. An

inner chord resounds. I
      play it
      again and
      again.

A Nod To Glenn Miller

Ballroom chandeliers and candy-colored streamers.
  —*Tell me, pretty girlie, whatcha doin' tonight?*

Pulled to the floor in perfect syncopation.
  —*Nothing could be better when you're feelin' so right.*

Cut a rug, bring back the good times.
  —*Keep that beat, that crazy rhythm.*

Roll back years to what we were—yeah,
  —*chuck your cares, you can't dance with them.*

Hear those horns drown out the drums. Hey,
  —*chase that trombone straight to the bar!*

In the mood—*ta-ra/ta-ra-ra*. Going far,
roll out that big band, for we're
steppin' out forever in a one-night stand.

Two In One

No space between twin cones
hanging as one on a single branch
of heavy-needled fir.
Sunset light throws perfect pink
on cylindrical shapes, highlights
every bract. Nothing lacking but
a satin bow to unify these two till
death.

Delightful to contemplate,
but too tightly bound for each
to swing divided in the wind,
to wear separate crowns of snow,
to drop freely their individual
seed, to be far enough away yet
feel unique
within the arm's long reach.

Tell It On The Water

Put your writing
on the water.
Tell me that you love me
like the fluid sun, and I
will feel secure
and rooted as the shrubs
and grasses,
knowing
that in interplay of light
there is
fast
sure
holding.

Respite On The Rogue

We came to the slumbering light of madrona
to put aside our clocks and gain time;
to see dusky red berries dropping one by one,
crackling soft seconds on a bank of oak leaves,
where acorns separated from protective crowns
are food for gray tails waiting in the pines.
Our slowed minds make slant discoveries;
observe the underside of locust leaves
veined in lemon light, trace rivulets of sap
like honey, sticky on the fingers.
We hold our breaths, aware we are part
of one portentous flaring
in this great gearing-down.

River Dream

From a hillside meadow trailing with cattle,
a rankling odor of dead skunk drifts over us. Whisps
of fog gauze flowering dogwood, each white bloom
a vibrato in forest song. On the river bank, droplets
of dew leave globes of light on thorny blackberry.

Trout elude all lines, wear
green tarnish reflected from burgeoning leaves,
slip into singing rapids.
We follow bright circles of sun, under the shadow
of a white crane's swoop into the spring-lit woods.

A blue triangle of sky startles the sun,
makes the wool scarves on our necks prickle. You
reach for my hand—a clammy encounter, until I am
certained by warmth kindling in your eyes.

A redtail hawk alerts us from the river's dream.
Our minds surface, become transfixed by fog vaporizing
through the trees,
ghosting us on an exit trail.

Ice Tree

Our copper beech tree froze last night—lofty branches
slicked by ice, old leaves encased in glass.

Coincidence that as the stately tree was freezing tight,
you and I, fighting stress, fell into a senseless argument.

Our pride set in as cold as ice upon that rigid tree.
We slept as separate as coffins, lined up side by side.

This morning's sun slants into stiffened branches, as
thaw comes on reluctantly, until a point of no return,

when showers of icicles break lose and clink and rain
like random diamonds round the rooted base below.

The brilliant air rings out with sudden breakage;
interjected laughter, mine, cuts in, as I

run under—pelted and released. You join me, grounded,
allowing all your pain to melt. Your laughter,
lifting high with mine, we bat at flying shards of ice.
In this chaotic hail, we let all the freezing go.

Unspoken Minds

Don't talk.
Let's just stretch out on this long couch
secured by big square pillows.
In reverse
like opposite ends of the same thought,
      your toes touch my arm,
         my feet press against your ribs.
Our breathing deepens,
becomes a rhythm for unspoken minds
like notes that flower—a flowing energy
of subtle hues, the color of new growth.

I sink in your sun-warmed fragrance,
      holding scent of newly mowed grass,
         travel to the vague outspace of thought.
We double as one, partners in a lengthening dance.
No words between us,
      just feelings,
         weightless, unbound.
In this channel of shared silence,
to feel is to know.

Winter Adagio

Frozen deep

a slow thaw's

coming...not

    to rolling overtures

    from Brahms

but ushered by stretched adagios,

    getting there

in slower measure.

Frozen deep,

thawing comes from bone.

The heart is wary of its hurt,

    announcing

    its arrival

in surer pace of stretched adagios.

Brahms For Breakfast

She wakes, ready for an undraped sun,
steaming coffee, and a bit of Brahms—
the Fourth, precisely.
He is one for silence,
Please pass the milk, and, certainly,
no need for Brahms.

As day builds, he gains momentum—water heater
won't fire, a trip to the hardware—no time
to settle until the desert sun cools,
and he hears the soft adagio of mourning doves
at vesper.

Together they watch the sun lower
behind the Rincon mountains, bare
and furiously magenta.
For her, the Fourth returns, in shadow sweep
across the undulating sand.
For him, a flaming meteor blasts into
the indigo of desert seas.

Rhythms build between them, compelling
as wind-whipped palms, fanning
final moments of light to a finale
booming from the black bass call of night.

The Ballad Of Wrangler Joe

Wrangler Joe, an old crust I knew,
was a banjo playin' fool.
His hair was white, his moustache, too;
'neath bushy brows, his eyes were blue.

Now Joe was smart, he followed his heart.
He told his lovin' wife,
"We must depart this city life;
let's leave this toil and strife.

"We'll head for mountains, desert, sea;
we'll travel far and free.
Sit by my side, my new-found bride,
and enjoy a thrillin' ride."

Those two set out with a whoop and a shout
in a trailer and a truck.
Old wrangler Joe, with his woman in tow;
he was bound to try his luck.

Across the land they traveled light;
they slept under starry nights,
where coyotes howl by a campfire's glow,
and midnight comes on slow.

It's there you'd find old Wrangler Joe,
his voice so deep and strong,
as he strummed his wanderin', travelin' song
on his trusty old banjo.

Well, the years rolled on as years will do,
and folks were sure they knew
that Wrangler Joe was dead and gone,
and his woman must be, too.

But others swear they're still out there,
that freedom lovin' pair,
for they can hear on lonely nights,
far from the city lights,

the clean, clear strum and the happy hum
they heard so long ago,
from the shadowy form of Wrangler Joe
and his ghostly old banjo.

Your Song, Once More

The song you sang to me
        when your voice was high and silky
lifted me higher than any fine elixir.
        Those roughened tones I hear today
stir in me now a tenderness.
        You raise my being to where I touch
your inwardness.

Then sing to me once more,
        and once again, for I hear sweeping
winds that batter the long climb
        up the canyon, once

only painted in the distance.

One Japanese Maple—Not For Sale

Twenty years ago you could have sold
the Japanese Lace Leaf Maple for fifteen
hundred dollars, but you chose not to.
"It adds value to my life," you said.
I know how much a part of every tree and shrub
you have become. Together, you and the Lace Leaf
add more gnarls each year to buffet hostile winds.

In deference to age, the tree kneels low, while
you spend winter, mostly reading in your chair.
This afternoon, an autumn crown sends
shivers of red onto our dining room walls,
transforming beige to hues of copper/pink.
The pruning you gave the tree in June has healed,
and sent new strength for October's brighter burning.

In spring, frail fingers will uncurl, etch
their signature on cobalt blue, inviting you
to go to the old greenhouse for the rusty rake
to work at the stubborn earth around the thawing
base, allowing metal teeth to do their grooming.

Watching from the window, I feel a cold draft
glance off the glass. I cannot help shudder
at the thought of your value diminished
by the maple's future loss, or the tree's by yours.

III *Meandering Muse*

$\mathcal{K}$eeping to the main road is easy,
but people love to be side-tracked.

Lao Tzu
570-490 B.C.

Sundial

An unmarked road leads me

to an old Saguaro   its

arms signal STOP   all I

can think of is that

it takes 75 years for

              this prickly hermit

to grow an arm   I

am not there yet

in the 100-degree heat

I hang a bad year   on

a sharp spine

look up the sides

              of the old recluse

and see its short shadow

has become a sundial

              fingering

almost noon

John Steinbeck's Salinas Valley

You wrote in exile, a native son rejected;
>   but never could they take this valley from you, Steinbeck,
>   this lucid valley of the Salinas,
>   its sweet wine grapes hedging scrub oak and cottonwood
>   shadows along the riverbed's moist spring banks,
>   where wind's strummed music sends tremolos
>   into just-green leaves.

Born in this lush land, you penned the lives
>   of dust-blown Joads, of migrant souls who plucked
>   more beans in a half hour than earned nickels in a day.
>   (The tale persists, of greed in the fields—rows and
>   rows, sweet in tended earth, turned acid in migrant
>   mouths; of workers still using hoes, squatting, stooping
>   in defiant competition with machines—a wrath that burns
>   like the blister of summer sun angered by its own heat.)

Valley patriots scorned your tales of fetid canneries:
>   the rankle of machinery over human belt lines,
>   of swollen fingers, split and bleeding,
>   of faces profiled in steamy shadows;
>   of hearts whose gears were slowly stripped—all
>   in the name of the great silver haul mined by nets
>   from the cache of Monterey Bay.
>   By the trillion they hailed—phosphorescent sardines,
>   fished in the dark of the moon. . .

Whistle blasts enslaved a polyglot parade into steel
>   belt lines, to labor in slime for periodic pay.
>   Decades...until slowly, very slowly,
>   the   fish   just   ran   out.

Into the abandoned waterfront
        came scavenger cats, winos and drifters.
        Fires blazed, reduced the cannery mile to a segment,
        which now lies like an embalmed corpse in a garish
        casket, viewed by circling gawkers—a new trap
        fashioned on encrusted pilings, a foundation
        on whose fallen backside the sea slaps a hard memory.

Your anger, Steinbeck, imprinted in a legacy among
        the lost—a forged irony; your wrath retracted like
        branches of scrub oak, jerking out, then pulling in.
        Was your release finally in velvet slopes you likened
        to heaven's pastures?

Diffused in salt mists, you ghost this country;
        the Joads, Doc, and Flora trailing with you, deep
        into layers of dawn fog which settles over
        criss-cross ranges: your essence in wounds made
        by setting sun's split light, bleeding purple
        and watering the earth with gold.

Your night over the soft Lucias' finds solace in
        raised arms of eucalyptus penciling across dark scrolls;
        your spirit heard in sighs from the Gabilans heaved
        at the sea, drawn into the pull of the tides—primordial
        pull of the soundless void.

Open Window In Bear Country

The bear at Glacier Park
came close enough to the trailer
window to sniff what was cooking.
He stood up on hind legs so I could
see the shine of his nostrils,
then he hunkered back down
and swayed from side to side
down the path, the black fur of his rear
glinting in the morning sun.

I guess he didn't like oatmeal!

Columbia Ice Fields
double cinquain

Finger

a rock,

trace running veins

up glacial ribs,

to vast moraine's blind light,

down the scoured rivers;

to see from every perspective,

hear the drops through the centuries—

witness

rebirth.

Photographer's Luck

Before the turn of the century
pioneer photographer, Peter Britt, took
the first picture of Crater Lake in Oregon.
It took him five days to do it:
      Five days going, five days back,
      and two days waiting for the right exposure.

It took me over an hour to do an autumn
close-up of some leaves in Lithia Park:
      Thirty minutes to pick the right leaves—
      a big red, a yellow maple, a toasted oak;
      twenty minutes to convince the ducks
      I wasn't going to feed them.
      Another ten to wait for a passing cloud,
      and a few moments more to meter in
      the right exposure.

Then carefully, patiently as Britt, I lowered
the leaves into the dappled water—red, gold, toast—
spaced precisely apart. A few more seconds
for the perfect focus—Aha!
      What? It cannot be!
      My practiced eye met only water.
      No leaves! They had slipped completely from view,
      sucked in by the drainpipe hidden under
      rocks beneath me.

It took Peter Britt twelve days.
At least he got a picture.

Celebration At Going-To-Sun-Mountain
with thoughts of Tiananmen Square, June 5, 1989

Summer hasn't been long
    at Glacier National Park. Alpine fir
    slide behind tall shadows in a fall down rocky
    cliffs, are caught by a glacial snow bank that
    lips around a palette of brilliant flowers:
    blue harebell, yellow snow lily, Indian paintbrush,
    and among these, the not-so-sweet bitterroot and
    yarrow.

Blue foreign car stops to praise the scene.
    A slight man and tiny son jump out.
    The father gives a whoop and leaps into
    the waves of color, lifting the boy's arm
    like a kite. They run for Going-to-Sun, heads
    raised to the stinging fragrance of the meadow.
    The boy jumps unevenly; blossoms rise to decorate
    his oval chin, leave petals on his dark round head.
    Father and son are swallowed by a field of light,
    dwarfed by the looming wall of the mountain.

In the car, the mother sits like a protective bear,
    with younger cub watching; until she can't restrain
    in high-pitched Mandarin that sings
    over the field, joins the song of a meadow lark.
    Like an alerted buck, the father bows his head
    as if he hears; then turns back—shirt open,
    hair wet on his forehead. As they approach the car,
    their steps slow. They are laughing. The boy's arm
    drags like a loose sleeve.

Observations While Climbing The Bighorn Mountains

Our trailer labors up the wall of a mountain,
We observe the press of eons on towering canyons.
"Rocks up to a billion years old," says the sign.

It's one thing to enjoy the scenery, but quite
another to get stuck behind a rusty cattle
trailer hauling four weighty cows. Swaying
precariously, the driver ruts into the gravelly
shoulder, hailing us with pellets. Eight pairs
of eyes stare balefully.

Nothing to do but ride inside the double yellow line,
watch the sun turn to rain, then back again.
Forests rush us from the river's edge—creation
rings in miles…and the cattle mouth their moos,
though we cannot hear them.

Tedium breaks through the side-view mirror
when a Type-A vacationer screams by
in a low gray sports car, over the double yellow,
past the baleful cows…and gone!

Did he see the monolithic red rock fingers
balancing infant formations on their tips?
Smell new sap from the trees?
Extend his hand to feel icy run-off gushing
down the canyon?

Did he hear the emerald leaves of aspen shivering?
Did he even notice four captive cows knocking into
one another in the beat-up rusty trailer?

The Great Sand Dunes

National Monument, Colorado

Where wind, river, mountains and sand converge,
ancient erosive forces built a range
of towering dunes in sifting windward surge,
up seven hundred feet, to rearrange
a wall of mountains in marriage to a sea
of displaced sand—a shimmering mirage,
which startled Indian dwellers—a mystery
and holy place, where caprice seems in charge.

What's alien often comes with offerings
that challenge and astound our finite minds,
presents us with rare influence and brings
an unveiled treasure to which we could be blind.
Great Sand Dunes power up and seek to gain
creation in disparate terrain.

The Old Coin Collector

A bright blue cap says "U.S.Navy".
He must have been an old salt in his day;
could now be in a nursing home—he's frail enough,
but has become a fortune-hunter along the way.
Metal detector clutched in shaky right hand
and a wood-handled screwdriver in the other,
he curves right over, listens to the telling beep
for trove he'll have to feel for in the desert sand.
Over thick spectacles he probes with his compulsive nose,
detects a beer can tab, and flings it high
in a meteoric spin, then looks for better treasure.
The old collector hears the beep once more
and hunkers down in ritualistic pose.
Sure fingers scratch; he stops and frowns, then
brings a crusty penny up—an Indian Head perhaps?
Unruly whiskers shield a roguish smile.
He stuffs the penny in his drawstring pouch
and ponders for awhile.
Then uncurls stiffly from a crouch,
and swerves on down the path, unrushed,
a fortune in his bag.
In letters tall and white,
his bright red blazer brags:

      I HIT A ROYAL FLUSH
      THE OTHER NIGHT
      IN LAUGHLIN, NEVADA!

Beyond The Desert's Eye

The desert broods over its infinite horizon.
No paths, trails, trees or wooden rails
restrain the gusty sage.
Prickly as cactus, hostile
as a scorpion's sting, yet gentle
as a breath of lavender at sunrise
and splendid as brass at sunset;
in rich color and uncontrolled

the desert calls, uninterrupted, for
an abandoned palette, for
tearing winds respecting only power, for
vegetation, shallow-rooted, dried
and tumbling in the flow,

like thoughts unleashed
over the plains of mind, unconstrained,
except for barriers of self
that feed on sure control, and, frightened,
reach for corners on plains that know no
bounds...

The letting go is hard.
Compulsions dictate order; yet
slow erosion, borne by winds and glaring
plains
like glass miraging on the mind,
brings on release that spreads
a desert honey, desiccated
from fields of sage,
distilled and on the sweeter edge
of sun and sand

on the far side of the desert's eye.

Haiku

Rocking in high wind,

mourning dove's nest in palm tree—

the cradle will fall.

. . . .

Winds parch desert night;

a scant drop of dew dances

on moon-blanched poppy.

Half A Prize

Rush for the sand dollar

buried on the shore,

stumble to your knees

    and create

    an explosion

    of flying diamonds.

Reach

    for the perfect disc

    that turns out to be

    a broken half!

West Of The Haraquahala Plain

The Eagle Tail Mountains rise west of the Haraquahala Plain.
Young, pinched, sawtoothed, and blue as lead, they reign
over the blowing sand.

Hearts of pioneers pulsed like gold nuggets here. Under
    shimmering noons, they rode like thunder
    to tame the land, all the while stoking
    inner fires. The hotter they burned, the more
    they thrived.
Palpable under nights showering stars and new moons,
    their dreams grew like prairie grass,
    in homesteads, cattle trade, and mining—
    ruled by guns and lynchings.
They ruled hard for more than a half century, before
    their dreams fluttered like lace petticoats,
    high over bawdy balconies, steaming bars and gunfire.
A few names remain—Old Camp, Coyote Wash, Burr Sage Ranch;
    and the brick foundations of scattered homesteads,
    rotted corral posts, rusted troughs, and tatters
    of Arizona cowhide tying history to an accountable
    wind, to the brittlebush, cholla and giant saguaro.

In a gas station off I-10, an old cowpunch named Bill
stares unwaveringly under thick red brows.
"My granddaddy homesteaded there." He points to the
base of the Eagle Tail Mountains.
    "He rode them mountains. Desert was his kin.
    Then everything went soft, and blowed away."
Bill gestures toward the lead-blue mountains, the windswept
plain, the tossed burr sage, and red-lipped ocotillo.
For a moment he listens to the howl of the wind, then,
    "Ain't much left." He spits hard, away from the
    surging air.
Banish the ghosts, the gas station, and long strip of I-10,
leading to Phoenix and that's all there would be:
The Eagle Tails resting, west of the Haraquahala Plain.

A Branch To Brace A Fishing Pole

Over Sisters
     black clouds linger.
Vine maple
     fiery over granite,
thunder splits
     the mountain,
hail shatters like broken glass.

On the road to Bend
     sun combs yellow
over fields
     and warms.

Ground squirrel
     burrows below
the frost line,
     comes
to a pool in the rock
to drink

The eye stretches across
     the river, listens
to water gliding a clear,
     continuous tape.

Someone has left a branch
     to brace
a fishing pole.

     Tonight
a snow white moon
     will light
the silence.

Oregon High Country

We camp in rugged Tumalo
  and rediscover truths we know:
Balance can't be forced. There is a flow,
  in everything, a come and go.

The beauty of each rock is singular
  when day cuts Vs into dark corridor,
and big white-petalled clouds rise up to flower
  above the woodsmoke in the conifer.

It's clear we dare not blame existence here:
  the short-lived June bug knows the calendar;
a ground squirrel on the run respects his fear,
  coyotes howl from far and near.

Summer is offset by winter's blow,
  the wind's both soft and harsh, as is the snow;
pale copper hues, green sage and silver glow,
  harmonious blending, rhythms high and low.

We stand apart and feel our oneness grow,
  as tension-free, a balance starts to show:
some values keep and others throw,
  we blend with cliffs above and earth below.

Our senses sharpened by an evening fire,
we watch the stars fall through the juniper.

A Train Trip To Copper Canyon
Lo que el tiempo se olvidó—What time forgot

Mother of mountains, Sierra Madre,
      when the flowers of the Palo Amarillo fall,
the leaves will come. My mind
      is clear, detached, at 8000 feet,
in the land of the Tarahumara, above
      the kapok trees.

The canyon opens a valve into the heart
      of the mountain and reaches mine—an entry
into deepest openings.

Is this surge of power inner or outer?
      Is the force continuous, weaving top
to bottom, side to side? I am
so close to knowing and not knowing.
I see a river clearly,
      but where the light shines, darkness
overcomes, in a long tunnel that slashes
      through stone, as we ascend to where
eagles circle clouds, and blue is blue.

Below the purple bougainvillea, langorous
      over adobe huts, water trickles
from sheer rock, moistening a serpentine
      cactus bonding itself to the cliff.

Beyond the village, an abandoned freight
      is home for families who live and die
within its iron confines. Only
      the river changes.

High in the canyon, the Tarahumara women
      have woven their baskets in precisely the
same way for thousands of seasons, certain
      as stars that rain over their caves.

Someone has crafted a cross from two pieces
        of pipe wedged on the face of a smooth boulder.
As the train creeps past, I wonder if the symbol
        prevails over lightning storms that split
tree from tree, over catapult of water
        that smooths the canyon walls;
and in summer over the sun's great unmercy.

Or, is this a part of that unfathomable force
        we call life, masked as kindly sufferance,
but ruddered by the same random power I am
        too compromised to comprehend?

Yet, on the far side of that hill
        wild horse sentinals watch over
a field of corn. Jolted by their
        beauty, I wonder if a scene like
this beckoned to John Keats.

The sweetest apples in Mexico doze
        among reaching pines, blinded by
sun and bitten by winds, a sweetness
        rendered by adversity—the force
of contradiction that sparks existence.

Before this track was built, only
        the canyon existed. I circle back
to the starting place, and cannot see
        beyond rims of stone, but reach

for clouds that blend me into syllables.

Shenandoah
Daughter of the Stars

High winds have hit, transformed
the trees to sputtering candles.
Toy villages and torched maples lie below.
Layered rocks give truth to glacial flattening—the
rise, the fall, the swinging doors of the Blue Ridge
Mountains, the weeping trail of Shenandoah,
daughter of the stars.

Indian warriors, cut from stone, stare blindly
at leafy spectres—the Blue, the Grey—in drummed
procession.

Thirteen decades past, the clash of thunder tore
these winding woods, as brothers bled upon the beauty
of this place, perished at Fisher's Hill, then east
at Menassas, south at Fredricksburg, and marched
with Sheridan and Stonewall Jackson.

Entombed in perpetual winter, leaden hearts beat
in vaulted skyline of the Shenandoah.

History is entrapped in burning autumn paths, chants
choruses to those who died, recharges our aching
souls in blend of remembered gunfire and muted,
peaceful haze of   blue   and   grey.

Shen-an-do-ah, daughter of the stars
hurries in the dusk.

En Camino A Taos
On the road to Taos

Se ven las chollas con
flores rosas, el aire
azul, las piedras
blancas, la tierra roja,
y la lucha clara como el
agua del Nambe, donde
nada se hace oscuro.

Un cielo sin nubes
en el valle del Rio Grande.
Un verde recién nacido amanece.
Se oyen en el viento entre los
arboles cuentos ancianos
de sufrimiento de conquis-
tadores que marchaban debajo
un sol duro.

Lágrimas secas como esta tierra
que baila cuando las nubes se
hinchan; el relámpago caí y el
mundo tiembla con los sacudos
de los truenos.

Aquí se engordan solamente
las truchas con ojos de plata.

Alguien a plantado una cruz
en las rocas altas.

Cuando paso, bajo la cabeza.

You see the rose-flowered
cholla, the blue air,
white rocks, red earth,
and the struggle, clear
as the waters of the
Nambe, where nothing is
obscured.

A cloudless sky in the
valley of the Rio Grande.
A newborn green appears.
You hear ancient tales
in windblown trees,
of the suffering of
conquistadores who marched
under a hard sun.

Dry tears, like this land
that dances when clouds
swell; lightning falls and
the world trembles with
the shaking thunder.

Here, only trout with
silver eyes grow fat.

Someone has planted a cross
in the high rocks.

When I pass, I bow my head.

Towers Of Zion

"All things change, nothing perishes." —Ovid

The canyon folds the past into the narrow night
    of its brain.
Fissured light stages a cast of players on brick-red
    stage.
They move. Hardened flesh returns to sinew,
    soft in the ruby dark.
A muscled form pulses in the clay, reaches to embrace
    a supple dancer.
They rope together, caught in a syllable of light.

Above them, a battle explodes.
    Mouths open, warriors sprawl in pools of blood.
On patriarchal walls, virgin fires burn like
    ebony on crystal.

A cold wind keens a child's cry from caprice
    of small bodies tumbling on the edge
of a pink escarpment.

Drop by drop, water cuts sandstone niches. Leaves
    its word.

From the shadows, a woman in milk-blue comes,
    carrying a basket of nectarines on her head.
She vanishes into the cleavage, with
    the dancers,
        the warriors,
           and the children
turned   to   stone   on   the   pink   escarpment.

Under a noon glare, a percipitous break
    on the canyon's face.

IV *Secrets From The Earth*

Vision is the art of seeing things invisible.

> Jonathan Swift
> Irish Satirist
> *1667-1745*

1. *A Hesitant Revelation*

$\mathcal{W}$e are driven to find the whole…

Secrets Of The Chiracahuas

A curved moon dishes stars
over the Chiracahuas
on to the glittering sand.
Coiled tight under rocks
wintering vipers sleep.
Howl of coyotes jars
a silence entombed
in the coral clasp of canyons.

Dawn bleeds over our dig.
The shard we unearth is faded,
except for burnished hieroglyphics,
where fire left its incantations.
We are driven to find the whole,
        each flawed piece—a
        hesitant revelation—its

first wash
in the sweat of our palms,
its shine
in dark moons of our eyes.

Do No Step Between The Bricks

My cat sits
                by the window
        on a patch of sun.

Brushing the pane
                the vermillion wings
        of new maple
                bead with dew.

New grass trembles.

Starlings peer
                from the bare crotch
of a gum tree.

Eager to finish
                new nests, they pitch
        their whistles high.

The challenge today
                is not to step
        on purple shooting stars

growing in bright moss
                between the bricks
of the old walk.

A Darkbellied Womb

We Give everything, including our lives. —Buddist Saying

Through The Window
rain drops on a nest
of trees, wet earth
steams its brew
        of rotting leaves,

acorn shells, and
lichen flourishing like sea life
on fir bark

        In a world inside the window you sit,

                                hands on your
                                belly
                                nourishing
                                a seed pod that has
                                taken hold in soft
                                walls of your womb.
                                You are daughter.
                                You are mother.

        In symbiosis,

roots transfuse
moisture to spores
on underside
of fronds.   Veins fill out
                                placental
                                fruit.

        In communion of water   and blood,
fir sucks
its rotting
nurse tree.   fetus swings
                                from mouth
                                of its umbilicus.

86

Only
eyes in the brush
reflect
the leaf
that moves like a heartbeat   in   a   graying   wind.

Above
the nest of trees
a caul of mist

a darkbellied womb   the stars.

Pioneer Cemetery At Tygh Valley

After a heavy rain, the McAtees, Smiths, and Conleys
        lie under tombstones,
        drowning in overflow
        of an irrigation ditch.

White picket gate, plastic flowers in garish glimmer
        catch the eye of a pregnant cow,
        her bulge heavy on soft grass,
        her sentinel gaze over barbed wire fence.

Two deer run across the road, come to the ditch
        to drink, nose the sacred script
        in soft massage of cherished names.

Mother quail and four chicks skitter into dry brush.

From the garbage cans of the old fairgrounds
        up the road,
        the clatter of   4   cats   dancing.

Daylight Savings Time
double cinquain

After
he sleeps all day,
hidden between old boards,
the spider returns to his web
and waits.
Whether
it's six o'clock
at night or seven by
daylight savings, it's all the same
to him.

Ethel By The Pond

Death rang no bells for you,
nor did you hear
the snapping bones
pile up on darkened step.

Scattered over trout pond,
your ashes form an opalescent caul
that mystifies the fish.
They've waited days for your return—
familiar shadow signalling their food,
gifting slurped kisses
on your phantom fingertips, their
global eyes mirroring a scattering of mustard,
lavender trees, pungent greens,
and your perfect grin.

(One afternoon we shared a pot of soup—onions, spicy
broccoli—warmed the dull green tones
of kitchen walls. And later,
Larry gave us rides on his proud tractor,
at least five years before he turned
to the recliner.)

Oh, Ethel,
you form a constellation
with your poems—clear moons alive with stars—
there'll be no burning of your words.

2. *The World on Hold*

*R*oll on, thou deep and dark
    blue ocean, roll!
Ten thousand fleets sweep over
    thee in vain;
Man marks the earth with ruin—

Lord Byron
1788-1824
Childe Harold's Pilgrimage

Beverly Beach, Three Decades Later
1965-1995

The world seems to have been on hold at
this Pacific shore. There, the same familiar
spit, where young ones splash in shallows, and run
to mountains of driftwood, stacked high for climbing.

The children are the ones remembered—a tummy hanging
over red trunks, a bright-haired daughter building
a city of sand, an older sister kicking up
a gleeful spray beyond the
water line.

Not a whisper of wind disturbs
the azure surf. Waves bring in the tide—
a-coming-in-a-going-out. Hidden deeply in the
water, unseen mercury churns its slow poisoning.

Over the tops of swells, scores of salmon glint no
more on their return to rivers, leaving their
spawns of silver. Gulls scavenge the beach
in scattered flight, but cormorants and
guillemots from the bird refuge are
gone. Where are the sanderlings
that used to race here by
the hundreds?

Children's voices ride
over the singing tide, are lulled
by its harmony. The spray that salts
their mouths tastes pure as ever. Gulls
shadow low over beach debris. A lone hermit
crab scurries to safety in an abandoned shell...

Bird Refuge At Arch Cape

Since the wildlife found here cannot endure human interference,
the refuge is closed to the public.   —Theodore Roosevelt

The birds churn in the waves at Arch Cape,
    ride on sea power,
duck under waves,
        fly, fish and breed, protected
        on rocks of a prison citadel.
Hunters, downwind on the Bayocean Spit
reach out with guns.
A bullet with eyes of its own
explodes in the watery dawn,
shatters the breast of a flying peregrine;
    he drops on the leaden arm of the spit,
    his 100-foot dive aborted,
    reduced to a pile of trembling bones,
    in a shroud of feathers.
Refuge rocks stand behind, heavy as tombstones.

But the mouth of the sea never closes.
It gushes its brine over rocks,
    remakes itself in each wave,
leaps at eggs nurtured in stony nests,
    uncurls starfish,
    transforms their orange eyes,
    in ink-blue water,
and stirs a brew of creatures crawling
at the bottom of its salted floor.

The day burns long in the tides.
At sunset, birds fly back to the refuge rocks.
Night folds over,
    the sea kicks a full moon over the breakers
    and sends it skipping like a gold tooth.
From the tall rocks, the night calls of peregrines,
    cormorants, grebes, guillemots...
Below them, the seaweed breathing.

A Threatened Species

The complex issue of the spotted owl,
endangered species in old forests West,
is viewed as logger pitted against fowl,
decried by woodsmen as a cruel jest,
a threat aimed at their very livelihood.
They rise against proposals that will ban
the means to earn their shelter and their food.
Is mottled bird worth more than needy man?

Meanwhile, the spotted owl flies not too far
from protests rocking the old timber mills.
His feathers puffed with down, his head ajar,
he searches tiny mice on which he fills,
his fate ensured by existential bliss,
protected by its ontogenesis.

Leave Nothing Brittle

The quality of mercy is not strain'd,
It droppeth as the gentle rain from heaven…

William Shakespeare
The Merchant of Venice

The rain has quieted me
    from a too-bright day
    of discord.
Rain leaves nothing brittle.

It soothes round scars
    oozing from a just-pruned Deodora.
    The tree lived one hundred years
to be insulted by a chain saw.

Likewise, our verbage buzzed,
    sawing off contested view points,
    trimming the reach
of proud perspectives.

Reconciliation drips cool drops
    down the window panes,
    in a gradual warming
from the inside.

The rain has quieted us
    from a too-bright day
    of discord.
Rain leaves nothing brittle.

Moonrise In A Blue Sky

Snow turns silver, dims the morning moon.
Under a drape of rain, ice bevels
the windshield. Mist tosses
rainbows on the road. Sun.
Plops of snow on teasel.
You say, "Around here
you get weather in
a fast punch."

Only in spring the yellow-green valley,
the purple lupine and riotous
mustard, wreathing groves
of cool eucalyptus.

A tape of Haydn plays on natural keyboard
of soft, chiseled hills—crescendos
climbing, 32nd notes trilling
from eroded gullies.

We slip into farmland. Miles and Miles.
Green on green. "I wouldn't want to
live here—too many chemicals,
toxic fertilizers…in the
water, too." Hard to
believe what is not
seen.

Don't the swallows know? They have
cemented their civilized nests
on the underside of
overpasses.

What of the blue heron, the white
crane, serene in waters of
the preserve?

On a blown fence, a crow stands still as
a black vase haloed by wild baby's
breath. Pure stars pulse
around its black shine.

A Sonnet To Unencumbered Growth

The sapling red-barked cedar must be moved.
The earth is moist now from the winter rain.
Five years ago its seed was volunteered
and settled where the parent tree had lain,
its trunk sawed into aromatic rounds.
Because the ancient pyramidal giant
obscured the garden path, the landscaped grounds,
its presence grew obtrusive, uncompliant.

Where seeds are sown is largely up to chance.
How fortunate when growth is guaranteed,
can override oppressive circumstance,
and gain great height from embryonic seed.
Yes, time to move the vigorous young tree
to woods where it can flourish, wholly free.

While Scaling The Salmon—Mozart's Concerto In C For Oboe

At first I am not aware I am being sustained
by the music: Tidy notes scale up and work back down.
Chop the head. Cut the tail. Remove the gills,
avoid the clouded eyes, and then begin to scale
what's left—a mere eight inches of mock form,
still seeming to swim in my hand.
My stomach tightens. Was this one small because
it couldn't swim to streams dried up by drought?
Would it have perished anyway?

Mozart holds the oboe's flawless climb to notes
as fine as hair. I am down to mottled gray.
Silver flakes pepper the cold sink, stick to my arms.
The smell of fish is fresh—forest air and cool streams.
            (I'll flour it well—plenty of dill and lemon-
            pepper; well-browned.)

The rubber form still in my hand, I raise my eyes
to the square window. Rain, finally. Everything leaden,
captured in a pale aquarium, except for
the bright leaf from the red vine maple
powered loose by the logical closures of Mozart.

Canyon Raid

He waters the young Pippin
in his garden. A net of
clouds floats over the sun.
Perhaps it will rain

Trapped in the canyon, a searing
wind hisses under a carrot-
colored sun, burns even the
jigger grass: Deer come down
each night to raid suburban
gardens.

A mind loosened by sleep,
he begins to dream; wakes,
peers into the restless dark,
returns to sleep…

The moon hides low in the trees.
Through a path of faltering pine,
deer follow stones of light, jump a
four-foot fence to the
garden. Reach for pears, silvered
by dawn, stretch hind legs to eat
moist leaves, evenly strip the
branches. They move to the
favored Pippin. Leave no cores.
Down tended rows of tomatoes,
juice dribbles from their velvet
mouths.

The sun patches its way to
his window. When he wakes,
the sky is fierce blue. He
rushes to water his garden
and meets the devastation.

All day he mourns—the tall
pears, tomatoes, the favored
Pippin. By midnight, his
rage has become a gun
pulsing in his hand.   The deer return at dawn,
                               a buck, two doe.

Gun raised, he watches their
smooth necks stretch for fruit
they missed. Dried leaves
shift under his feet. The
deer flash into a run. He
aims at a doe gliding over
the fence, her tail a flickering
talisman…He does not shoot.

The grass flattens under his
footsteps. He wonders how high
to build the fence…

3. *The Tide Knows*

$\mathcal{N}$othing is rich but the inexhaustible wealth of nature. She shows us only surfaces, but she is a million fathoms deep.

Ralph Waldo Emerson
Essays—1844

Slow Walk Through The Poplars At Gabriel Park

You and I are home among these poplars.
          Our minds unhinge,
          on full September
          tides.
Fly with familiar birds that stop
          in the same trees
          every year
          on their way somewhere
          south.

We turtle along the path,
          you, heavy with babe,
          I, with the complementary
          stride of grandmother.
Left and right, a high generation
          of poplars
          loses its leaves
          like confetti,
          over veridian banks,
leaving colored lanterns hanging everywhere.

The babe will come when its ready, you know,
          like a corn field
          ripe for picking,
          crackling in a blue wind,
or like the roses blooming furiously in your garden.

The tides know, and the moon,
          that pale boat
          we saw last night
with a whisp of cloud pushing
          like a sail, or
          the black crows,
silky in a breathless wind.

At the turnaround, light spikes
                the tree trunks,
                warms us, and we
look into each other's eyes: it's been a long wait.

In a few days robins will go giddy
                on red berries
                of the mountain ash;
                the moon will be
                full,
and the baby will come...you'll see.

Spring Brew

Skunk cabbage brews in the swamp,
its yellow ears listen for secrets
of growth in soft whine of cells,
as ferns uncurl and tendrils reach.

Green now, on the alder,
branches spider out to fir tips
that lift like cathedrals to the sun.

All paths run down to a resurgent line of waves:

> a brawny man loosens
> his dachsund to the water,
> and stands back, laughing
> at little brown head dancing
> like an otter in the foam.

> Woman in red Spanish skirt
> leaps at a ceiling of gulls.
> They dip and claw
> at her jumping hands, picking
> at bread stuck to her fingers,
> their pink legs, flashing
> rubber in the sun.

Once they are fed, the gulls float away like down.

> Unmindful, a small boy
> in a shirt too big
> digs like a pup in the sand.

The Whale-Watchers

a narrative poem

On the coast in spring when skunk cabbage shoots its
yellow ears, the gray whales migrate north for summer.

Whale-watchers follow their migrations at the lighthouse at
Cape Meares, where cliffs toe the ocean.

Watchers hang over rocks and scrutinize the sea, focus
beyond breakers for signs. They watch the tide push through
the doors of Arch Cape, listen to the thunder of waves
trapped in caves.

A man with a red beard cries, "There's a spout!"

But it's just another geyser in a rock.

Another hour and a petral surfaces.

"That's them!" Redbeard insists.

"Naw," a blue-capped friend replies, "but," touching his
intellectual nose, "they're out there, somewhere."

A baldheaded spectator joins them. He nods his approval.

In the third hour, silent as submarines, the whales arrive.

Redbeard slaps his thigh, "That's them! Just like
I seen 'em in California."

He squints. A half-mile away they spout, a gentle spray,
three or four feet, barely visible Their backs shine darkly
in the waves.

Baldhead shifts his weight. "I took a pitcher once.
You could only see black specks."

Further out, a few more spouts. The whales move on.

The watchers disperse, but the three men linger.

Blue-cap clears his throat. "Come on, let's go.
'A watched pot,' you know, or should I say, 'a watched whale
never spouts.'"

They all laugh—too loud.

Past a curve of trees, Redbeard stops for a last look.
"They sure come a lot closer in California."

Sea Music

Sun-filtered rain falls
soft as gold dust,
leaves pinpoints in the sand.

Walking alone,
a palsied youth makes
his discoveries, his eyes
freezing on a smooth-lipped shell.
Puppetlike,
he touches the shell,
fingers reach   jerk
tremble on the coral edge.

Head thrown back,
he twists a grin at the sky.
Bends. Pillows his ear,
listens
to the music of the sea.
        It sings to him
        of water sparkle,
        of green fire from mouths of fish,
        of soothing grains of sand
        moving loosely under seaweed.

Waving the shell in his fist,
he drags his legs to where
his friends are wading
in the shallow waves.

His Eye Is On The Sparrow

Caught in plastic twine
a sparrow hangs by one leg.
Blood pools
under the featherless skin
of its thigh.

I cup the injured bird
in the warmth of my hand.
He blinks.
Let's us know he's still alive.

Jane performs the surgery,
cutting strand by strand
with big scissors
she keeps in her car.

Free,
the bird flaps
onto a strip of daisy grass,
retreats to an umbrella
of leaves.

We would like to wait
to see it fly, but
it's not safe to park
on this busy highway.

St. Francis Of The Sea

Lover of sea birds,
restless waves and sun,
nothing brought by the sea
halts
this rover's vigil
by the shore.
Hair blowing, he rides
storms on petral wings,
vanishes
with fog at dusk.
Returns at dawn
with feet washed clean
to pick off purple mussels
from the rocks.

With splints of driftwood,
he sets the wings of wounded birds.
(Once, when moontide beached
a baby whale, he heard its call,
and rushed to pull its heavy body
back to sea.)

A San Francisco man who drifted in?
An ex-priest? Those
who've seen him close insist
he wears a sun-worn cross.

All anyone knows
is that he lives his days
by the tides.

Heavy over fishing nets
and beer, the townsfolk say
he'll disappear
the way he came—quickly
like a gale,
or following his own light,
step
into sunset fire,
and slip
like a clam through the tides.

Takeover
cinquain

Blue jays

plunder small nests

like big corporations

hoarding assets under greedy

wide wings.

Feast Of The Cedar Waxwing

When Bacchus calls on the cotoneaster bush,
a dozen cedar waxwings jounce on red berry boughs,
shoving like school kids in game of catch.

I become voyeur, eyeing an annual feast
as berry wine shapes its sorcery on each
courtly bird making forays to and from
the bush less and less discreet.

A spy behind glass, I peer with some degree
of glee as each breast fills smooth,
and birds turn tipsy on the boughs.
In perverse scrutiny, I wait to recognize
remorse in ever-glittering pairs of eyes—winking
rhinestones set in carnival masks, topped by
jaunty, crested caps.

Then raucous tumbling stops as if by magical command.
Yellow-tipped tails fan in volant readiness,
and flashing wings explode.

Abandoned,   .
I count   .
v a n i s h i n g   .
c   h   e   c   k   m   a   r   k   s   .

Death Of A Red-Barked Cedar In Oregon's 1995 Windstorm
villanelle

For eighty years the cedar lived in grace,
where other aging conifirs abound,
until a hungry wind consumed its space.

A devil wind brewed, in a hostile place
in ocean's depth, where mysteries resound.
For eighty years the cedar lived in grace.

The towering tree bore boughs of tight green lace
and offered nightly shelter raccoons found,
until a hungry wind consumed its space.

Thick branches torn apart in storm's dread pace,
the red-barked giant fell with windmasked sound.
For eighty years the cedar lived in grace.

Its trunk inert, its roots in feigned embrace,
lost to this garden, from the earth unbound,
because a hungry wind consumed its space.

Now part of nature's plan is to replace
a king of trees with seeds in nearby ground.
For eighty years the cedar lived in grace,
until a hungry wind consumed its space.

Euthanasia

Dry wind cauterizes aspen,
    seres leaf veins,
      cuts off feed lines,
provokes undisputed winter.

In slow bloodletting,
    each cell is allowed
      to die. Blinks shut.
Returns its color to earth.

Across the blowing sage
    a seed,
      unbidden,
wings on a death ride.

Falls.   Waits   for   snow.

Haiku

A gleaming trout

trembles the water apart—

a night of twelve moons.

East wind brings sunshine

and blows my beech tree's leaves

into my neighbor's yard.

Cactus Salute

With splendid proclivity
the Saguaro cactus plans its longevity:
By extending inches over patient years,
it equals the heights of its older peers,
towering straight at the sky,
fifty feet high!
Then at seventy-five, Saguaro proves
a healthy maturation
by sprouting arms, in mockery
of normal gravitation.

These prolific patriarchs
invest in firm fertility
by scattering millions of seeds
to insure their continuity.
Flowering brilliantly on summer nights,
white waxy blossoms burst like stars at play,
then slowly dim in sunset light
of one full day.

Although Saguaro is full of charm,
be wary of its angled arm,
lest you should place a treasured hat
and expect to get it back intact!
On the other hand, praise its beauty all you desire,
for flattery will never raise Saguaro's ire.

And when you photograph this great centurion,
take note of its wondrous constitution.
Look up, right where you are,
and shout to near and far,
"Tell me, pardner, if you can grow so long, so high,
improving growth with bountiful maturity,
pray, desert friend, why shouldn't I?"

Recipe From An Oyster

How do we adjust?

I think, like the oyster must:

Working our own elements

around gross irritants,

over and over,

creating new environments.

Where change is sown

new pearls are grown.

About The Author

Poet, artist, photographer and author,
Doreen Gandy Wiley was born in the
Philippine Islands and experienced the
holocaust of World War II in that country.
In her novel *Fires Of Survival*, published in
1995 by Strawberry Hill Press, she relates
the horrors of that experience. Many of her
poems in *Say The Silence* also reflect the
theme of survival in the face of adversity.

Retired from a teaching career as a
reading and writing instructor at Portland
Community College, Doreen continues to
be active on the literary scene as a writer
and advisor.